12-99

ook is due for return on or befo

Metals and Non-metals

DENISE WALKER

EVANS

LONDON

© Evans Brothers Ltd 2007

Published by:
Evans Brothers
2a Portman Mansions
Chiltern Street
London W1U 6NR

Series editor:
Harriet Brown

Editor:
Katie Harker

Design:
Robert Walster

Illustrations:
Peter Bull Art Studio
Ian Thompson

Printed in China by
WKT Company Limited

British Library Cataloguing in
Publication Data

 Walker, Denise
   Metals and non-metals. -
   (Science essentials. Chemistry)
   1. Metals - Juvenile literature
   2. Nonmetals - Juvenile literature
   I. Title
   546.3

ISBN-10: 0-237-53003-1
ISBN-13: 978-0-237-53003-7

Contents

Introduction

The different substances that surround us have very particular properties. Some materials are hard and dense while others are brittle and break easily. Some objects conduct heat and electricity very well while others are useful as liquids or gases. Thanks to the work of chemists, we now know more about the different materials in our world and how best to use these objects for our own needs.

This book takes you on a journey to discover more about the wonderful world of metals and non-metals. Find out what distinguishes a metal from a non-metal, discover the way in which metals are found and extracted and look at how we can refine materials to make them more useful. You can also find out about famous scientists, like Dimitri Mendeleev and Humphry Davy. Learn how they used their skills to make sense of the materials around us and to find ways in which different substances can be extracted.

This book also contains feature boxes that will help you to unravel more about the mysteries of metals and non-metals. Test yourself on what you have learnt so far; investigate some of the concepts discussed; find out more key facts; and discover some of the scientific findings of the past and how these might be utilised in the future.

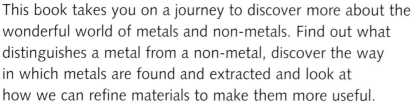

Metals and non-metals make up our world. Now you can understand why these materials behave in the way that they do, and how their properties are valuable to our everyday lives.

DID YOU KNOW?

▶ Watch out for these boxes – they contain surprising and fascinating facts about the metals and non-metals in the world around us.

TEST YOURSELF

▶ Use these boxes to see how much you've learnt. Try to answer the questions without looking at the book, but take a look if you are really stuck.

INVESTIGATE

▶ These boxes contain experiments that you can carry out at home. The equipment you will need is usually cheap and easy to find around the home.

TIME TRAVEL

▶ These boxes describe scientific discoveries from the past and fascinating developments that pave the way for the advance of science in the future.

ANSWERS

At the end of this book on pages 46 and 47, you will find the answers to the questions from the 'Test yourself' and 'Investigate' boxes.

GLOSSARY

Words highlighted in **bold** are described in detail in the glossary on pages 46 and 47.

Different types of elements

Since the very earliest times, humans have used a number of different materials to carry out their everyday tasks. The shiny substances that we call metals have been very important in shaping modern human civilisation because they can be used for construction, technology and transportation. Other, very different materials, such as liquids and gases, have a number of useful properties, too. Over the years we have learnt how best to use these materials for our own needs.

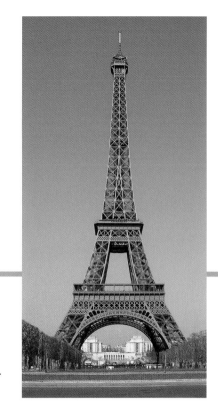

▶ The Eiffel Tower is made from iron. It is 300 metres tall and weighs over 10,000 tonnes.

WHAT ARE METALS?

All the objects that we see around us are made up of elements – basic substances that are composed of just one type of atom. Elements cannot be broken down into simpler substances, but they can combine to make different materials.

Metals are a class of materials that have unique and distinctive properties. Most metals are hard and **dense** – they cannot be scratched easily and they sink if they are put in water. Nearly all metals are solid at room temperature and it takes a great deal of heat energy to melt and boil them.

In contrast, non-metals are a class of materials with very different properties. Non-metals are less hard and dense, and some are liquids or gases at room temperature.

THE PERIODIC TABLE

We can use the **Periodic Table** (see page 8) to find the names of different types of elements. The format of the Periodic Table shows us that about two-thirds of elements are metals whilst one-third are non-metals. However, some elements demonstrate properties of both metals and non-metals. We call these elements 'metalloids'. In the Periodic Table they are found near to the dividing line between metals and non-metals. Silicon (Si), for example, has a shiny appearance but it is brittle and does not conduct heat or electricity as well as some metals.

◀ This sink is mostly made from metal, but the glass and the water are made from non-metallic elements.

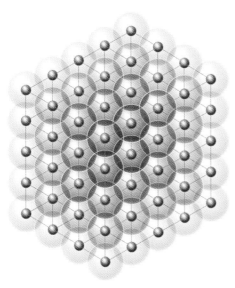

▲ This lattice structure is typical of the atoms in a metal.

THE STRUCTURE OF METALS AND NON-METALS

The properties of metals can be explained by the arrangement of their atoms. Metal atoms are held together in a regular 'lattice' structure – a very organised, symmetrical pattern. In this structure, the atoms become positively charged because they lose one or two **electrons**. These electrons travel around the structure and act like a kind of 'glue', holding the atoms together. In contrast, most non-metal **compounds** are a collection of just a few atoms. The electrons in non-metal structures are also not free to move around.

COMMON PROPERTIES OF METALS

Metals are usually:

▶ **Strong** – The atoms in metals are held so tightly together that they can withstand large forces without pulling the atoms apart.

▶ **Malleable** – Metals can be bent and hammered into different shapes without breaking. When a metal is hammered, the atoms are compressed closer together making the structure stronger.

▶ **Conductors of heat and electricity** – Some of the free electrons in a metal structure carry electrical charge and heat energy.

▶ **Shiny** – If metals are polished or freshly cut, their smooth surface reflects light very easily.

▶ Ductile – Most metals can be pulled into wires. The metal atoms are pulled into fine layers that are very strong. Copper, for example, is a **ductile** metal. It can be made into electrical wiring (below).

USES OF METALS

Metals are selected for different products according to their particular purposes. We do not use sodium metal for saucepans, for example, because it is soft and far too reactive (see page 18). Jewellery is usually made from gold or silver because these metals tend to hold their shine.

SOME IMPORTANT GROUPS OF METALS

In 1869, the first version of the Periodic Table was drawn up by the Russian chemist, Dimitri Mendeleev. Mendeleev based his organisation of known elements almost entirely on observation. He looked for particular patterns in the chemical reactions of elements and organised elements into vertical columns (which we now call groups). Elements in the same group have similar chemical and physical properties. They are not identical, but gradually change as you move through the group.

▲ Dimitri Mendeleev's Periodic Table is still used by chemists today.

THE PERIODIC TABLE

																	8
1 H																	2 He
3 Li	4 Be											5 B	6 C	7 N	8 O	9 F	10 Ne
11 Na	12 Mg											13 Al	14 Si	15 P	16 S	17 Cl	18 Ar
19 K	20 Ca	21 Sc	22 Ti	23 V	24 Cr	25 Mn	26 Fe	27 Co	28 Ni	29 Cu	30 Zn	31 Ga	32 Ge	33 As	34 Se	35 Br	36 Kr
37 Rb	38 Sr	39 Y	40 Zr	41 Nb	42 Mo	43 Tc	44 Ru	45 Rh	46 Pd	47 Ag	48 Cd	49 In	50 Sn	51 Sb	52 Te	53 I	54 Xe
55 Cs	56 Ba	57 La	72 Hf	73 Ta	74 W	75 Re	76 Os	77 Ir	78 Pt	79 Au	80 Hg	81 Tl	82 Pb	83 Bi	84 Po	85 At	86 Rn
87 Fr	88 Ra	89 Ac	104 Rf	105 Db	106 Sg	107 Bh	108 Hs	109 Mt	110 Ds	111 Rg							

Groups — 1, 2 ... 3, 4, 5, 6, 7

Atomic number (the number of protons contained in the atoms of each element)

Metals / Non-metals

58 Ce	59 Pr	60 Nd	61 Pm	62 Sm	63 Eu	64 Gd	65 Tb	66 Dy	67 Ho	68 Er	69 Tm	70 Yb	71 Lu
90 Th	91 Pa	92 U	93 Np	94 Pu	95 Am	96 Cm	97 Bk	98 Cf	99 Es	100 Fm	101 Md	102 No	103 Lr

GROUP 1 – THE ALKALI METALS

The first column in the Periodic Table is called group 1, or the alkali metals. The metals in this group are called lithium (Li), sodium (Na), potassium (K), rubidium (Rb), caesium (Cs) and francium (Fr). These elements display many of the properties not always associated with metals. However, we still consider them to be metals because they can conduct heat and electricity and have an extended structure.

PROPERTIES OF THE ALKALI METALS

The alkali metals are incredibly reactive and because they are chemically unstable they do not have many practical uses. We store these metals in oil because they even react with water in the air! The alkali metals should usually only be handled by your teacher, who may use absorbent paper to remove the oil, and then cut the metal into a manageable size. The metals are very soft so we do not use them to make structures and vehicles.

When alkali metals are placed in water, they react vigorously. Consider the photograph below of potassium reacting with water. How many different observations can you make?

▲ Potassium metal reacts very vigorously in water.

(1) The metal floats on the surface. The alkali metals are not very dense because their atoms are not packed as tightly together in the extended structure, as they are in other metals.
(2) The metal moves around as it reacts. The alkali metals will react with the first substance they come across – in this case, water.
(3) The metal forms a molten ball. The alkali metals have low melting points and the heat released from the vigorous reaction is therefore sufficient to melt the metal.
(4) A colourless gas is given off during the reaction. This gas is hydrogen.
(5) The hydrogen gas may ignite to produce a colourful flame. The reaction of alkali metals with water becomes more vigorous as you move down group 1. If sufficient heat is released (as it is with potassium, rubidium, caesium and francium) the hydrogen gas may ignite.

USES OF GROUP 1 METALS

Due to their unusual reactivity, group 1 metals do not have any direct uses, but their compounds have important uses in many everyday materials.

Lithium (Li) is used in certain medical treatments for depression, as well as in glass dyes and ceramics. Spectacles that react (and darken) in sunlight are rich in a compound called lithium carbonate. Lithium is also commonly found in batteries.

Sodium (Na) is common in the preservative and flavouring we call table salt (sodium chloride). It is also found in some medicines and in soaps.

Potassium (K) is found in some soaps and is also used as a substitute to the sodium in table salt for those on a low-sodium diet. Potassium is also commonly found in glass. It is used to make gunpowder and can be found in some fertilisers.

Rubidium (Rb) is found in fireworks (below) and in some photocells that convert sunlight into electricity. Rubidium is also used as a **catalyst**.

Caesium (Cs) is found in atomic clocks (precise clocks that are timed by the **radioactive** disintegration of caesium) and in photocells. Caesium also has some medical applications, such as in the treatment of cancer.

Francium (Fr) has no known uses because it is highly radioactive and chemically unstable.

THE TRANSITION METALS

Other important metals come from a horizontal block of the Periodic Table called the transition metals. These metals tend to be strong and do not **corrode** very easily. For this reason, they are often used in **alloys** (see pages 34-36). The transition metals include copper, iron and the modern metal titanium.

Titanium (Ti) is sometimes described as a modern metal because its uses and properties have only been recently exploited. Titanium is an expensive metal because its extraction from natural **ores** requires a lot of electricity. However, titanium is unusual because it has great strength as well as being very light. Titanium is suitable for sports equipment, such as tennis racquets and golf clubs, and is an ideal metal for building aircraft.

Copper (Cu) is used for electrical wiring and in water pipes. In Victorian England, original water pipes were made from a cheaper metal called lead.

TEST YOURSELF

▶ Explain why:
(1) Sodium is not suitable for metal saucepans.
(2) Titanium should not be used to build bridges.

Unfortunately, over a long period of time, small pieces of lead began to break off and contaminate the water, causing the public to be at risk of fatal lead poisoning. Many old lead pipes have gradually been replaced with the less harmful and completely un-reactive metal, copper. Copper also has the added advantages of being easily bent into shapes, whilst maintaining its high strength.

Iron (Fe) has been used for thousands of years for building, and to make weapons. In 1200 BCE, it was discovered that iron could be mixed with carbon to make it stronger (today, we call this metal the alloy 'steel'). Before long, this strengthened iron was used to make stronger, sharper swords to replace the traditional bronze swords used at the time.

◀ In the future, many bicycles will be made from titanium. The lightness of the metal will help the cyclist to travel faster.

SOME NON-METAL GROUPS

Another family in the Periodic Table is the halogens (or group 7). These non-metal elements include fluorine (F), chlorine (Cl), bromine (Br), iodine (I) and astatine (At).

PHYSICAL PROPERTIES OF THE HALOGENS

The halogens show chemical and physical properties that are in contrast to many metals. These elements are made up of diatomic molecules – they are found as pairs of atoms chemically **bonded** together. In equations, we write symbols of these elements with a figure 2 (for example, chlorine is written as Cl_2). The halogens have a simple molecular structure, in contrast to the extended structure of metals.

As you move down the group of halogens there is a gradual change in their properties. For example:

Halogen	Colour	Physical state
Fluorine (F_2)	Pale yellow	Gas
Chlorine (Cl_2)	Yellow / green	Gas
Bromine (Br_2)	Orange / brown	Liquid
Iodine (I_2)	Grey / black	Solid

The halogens become progressively darker and more solid as the group is descended. This is because the larger halogen molecules have a stronger attraction and sit closer together. Because metals have an extended structure, this variation in physical state and colour does not occur.

CHEMICAL PROPERTIES OF THE HALOGENS

We have seen that the alkali metals become more reactive as you move down the group (see page 9). However, the halogens become more reactive as you move 'up' the group. The most explosive reaction between an alkali metal and a halogen is between caesium (Cs) in group 1 and fluorine (F) in group 7 (in theory it would be francium (Fr) and fluorine but francium is rarely found in nature). Fluorine is the most reactive non-metal element – over time it will chemically attack glass.

USES OF THE HALOGENS

Due to their simple structure, non-metals are generally not suitable as strong building materials. However, the halogens have lots of other uses:

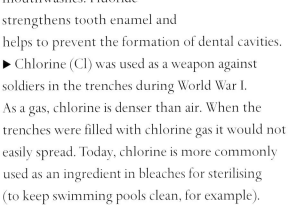

▶ Despite its high reactivity, compounds of fluorine (F) have a wide variety of uses. Fluoride is often added to our water supply and can be found in toothpastes (right) and mouthwashes. Fluoride strengthens tooth enamel and helps to prevent the formation of dental cavities.

▶ Chlorine (Cl) was used as a weapon against soldiers in the trenches during World War I. As a gas, chlorine is denser than air. When the trenches were filled with chlorine gas it would not easily spread. Today, chlorine is more commonly used as an ingredient in bleaches for sterilising (to keep swimming pools clean, for example).

▶ Bromine (Br) is used in the production of some medicines and pesticides. It is also commonly found as silver bromide in photographic film.

▶ Iodine (I) is used as an antiseptic. It can be easily recognised because it turns skin yellow!

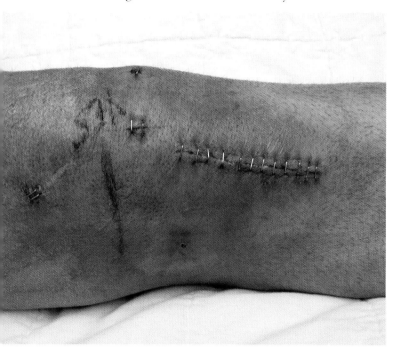

▲ This wound has been treated with iodine.

▼ The atoms in this gas move freely and fill the container.

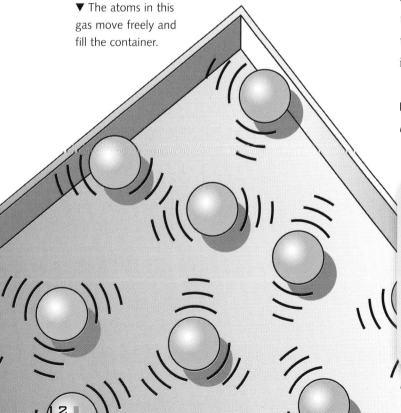

THE NOBLE GASES

Another important group of non-metals is the noble gases (or group 8). These gases have simple structures, with atoms that move around.

USES OF THE NOBLE GASES

The noble gases are extremely un-reactive, so they remained undiscovered for many years. However, they still have many uses:

▶ Helium (He) boils at -269°C so liquid helium can be used as a coolant. Liquid helium is used to cool machinery such as body scanners, for example, that need to be kept at low temperatures to work effectively. Helium is a very light and un-reactive gas. Because it is so much lighter than air, it is ideally suited to lift airships.

▶ In the 1800s, neon (Ne) was found to glow when placed under low pressure. This discovery forms the basis of the neon signs that we see today.

▶ Argon (Ar) is also a very un-reactive gas and is used to fill light bulbs. Argon will not react with the tungsten filament in a light bulb, even when it is white hot.

▶ Krypton (Kr) is used for the lasers that perform corrective eye surgery.

TEST YOURSELF

▶ Astatine (At) is the final member of the halogen group. It is very radioactive and samples do not last very long. In fact, it is very difficult to get enough astatine at any one moment to examine and test it. Using the elements found in the Periodic Table as a guide (see page 8), predict the colour and physical state of an astatine molecule.

Metal reactions

Experiments have shown that metals react with many different substances, such as oxygen, water and acids. Sometimes, these reactions can be a nuisance – causing our cars to rust or our silver to become tarnished. But metal reactions have their advantages, too. Metal reactions can be used for particular purposes (in the flash of a camera, for example) and they also form useful compounds.

REACTIONS OF METALS WITH OXYGEN

Many metals react with oxygen to form metal oxides. For example, aluminium is a reactive metal that will quickly react with oxygen in the surrounding air to form aluminium oxide. An equation for this reaction is:

Aluminium $+$ Oxygen $\longrightarrow$ Aluminium oxide

$$2Al_{(s)} + 3O_{2(g)} \longrightarrow Al_2O_{3(s)}$$

We call the materials present at the start of a chemical reaction (such as aluminium and oxygen) the 'reactants' and the materials present at the end of a chemical reaction (such as aluminium oxide) the 'products'. When equations like this are written down, we sometimes need to add numbers so that the equation remains balanced. This is because during a chemical reaction, the amount of atoms before and after the reaction stays the same. The letters in brackets show the physical state of the reactants and products. For example, (s) solid, (l) liquid, (g) gas and (aq) **aqueous** (dissolved in water).

TEST YOURSELF

▶ The reactivity of zinc (see page 18) is between that of magnesium and iron. Predict how zinc will react with oxygen and any notable observations. Write a word and symbol equation to represent this reaction.

Aluminium reacts very quickly with oxygen in the air, but other metals react much more slowly. Silver, for example, reacts with oxygen over a period of weeks. The silver will begin to lose its shine and is said to have tarnished. Only very un-reactive metals (such as titanium, platinum and gold) do not react with oxygen to form a metal oxide.

SOME METAL-OXYGEN REACTIONS

We have seen that some metals from the Periodic Table are very reactive. The alkali metals (see page 8), for example, react at room temperature. These metals are stored in oil to prevent them from reacting with water and oxygen in the air.

▲ Silver has to be polished regularly to remove its tarnish.

Sodium (Na), for example, readily burns in oxygen to produce sodium oxide:

Sodium $+$ Oxygen $\longrightarrow$ Sodium oxide

$$4Na_{(s)} + O_{2(g)} \longrightarrow 2Na_2O_{(s)}$$

An experiment can help to demonstrate this reaction – sodium is gently heated before being plunged into a gas jar of pure oxygen. The burning sodium produces a bright orange flame and at the end of the reaction, a yellow powder of sodium oxide is produced.

Some metals have less dramatic reactions with oxygen, but metal oxides can still be formed. Some other metal-oxygen reactions include:

Magnesium	Reacts quickly, emitting a bright white flame. Sometimes used in the manufacture of colourful fireworks.
Iron	Does not burn in oxygen, but will glow brightly when heated. The remaining black powder is called iron oxide (Fe_2O_3).
Copper	Does not burn in oxygen, but when the metal is heated it becomes coated with black copper oxide powder.

As you move down the table, notice how the metals used in these experiments have a less dramatic reaction with oxygen – the un-reactive metals do not react at all.

LOOKING AT THE PRODUCTS

An important skill in chemistry is to look at patterns in chemical behaviour and to use these patterns to predict behaviour about unknown substances. The reactions of metals with oxygen have one important pattern that is worth remembering for other metal-oxygen reactions. All metal oxides are bases. Some of the metal oxides will dissolve in water and turn a different colour when an **indicator** is added, showing that they are alkalis. In the examples here, sodium oxide is soluble and is therefore an alkali. Copper oxide is insoluble and is therefore a base. All alkalis and bases will react with acids.

DID YOU KNOW?

▶ A camera flash relies on a metal reaction. The basic parts of the flash are a small battery, a gas discharge tube filled with xenon gas and an electrical circuit that has a metal inside it. When the battery is switched on, a flow of electrons travels through the discharge tube and works its way around the electrical circuit. The xenon atoms become electrically excited by the presence of these electrons, causing them to emit energy in the form of visible light.

Old-fashioned flash bulbs did not have an electrical supply. Instead they relied on the combustion reaction of magnesium. The equation for this reaction is:

Magnesium + Oxygen ⟶ Magnesium oxide
$2Mg_{(s)} + O_{2(g)} \longrightarrow 2MgO_{(s)}$

This reaction gives out a bright flash of white light.

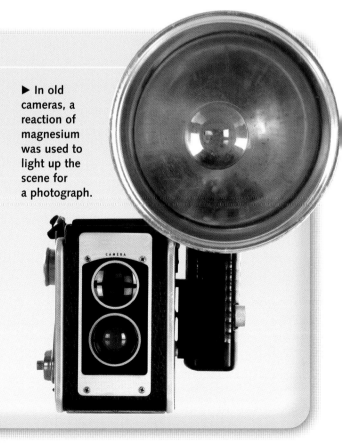

▶ In old cameras, a reaction of magnesium was used to light up the scene for a photograph.

REACTIONS OF METALS WITH WATER

In a similar way to metal-oxygen reactions, the reactions of metals with water will also vary gradually according to the reactivity of the original metals. The alkali metals, for example, react instantly and vigorously, whereas the reaction of iron to form rust is a much slower process.

▶ **Sodium** reacts violently with cold water – it moves randomly across the surface, forming a molten ball before disintegrating. The equation for this reaction is:

Sodium ✚ Water ⟶ Sodium hydroxide ✚ Hydrogen

$$2Na_{(s)} + 2H_2O_{(l)} \longrightarrow 2NaOH_{(aq)} + H_{2(g)}$$

Sodium hydroxide is soluble and dissolves in the water. It also turns universal indicator purple because it is a strong alkali. Hydrogen gas is also produced during the reaction.

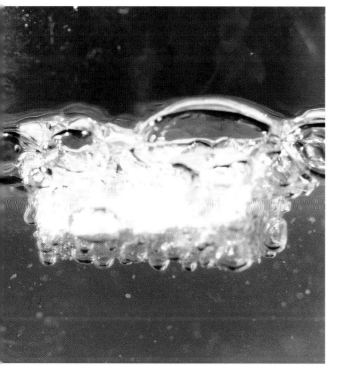

▲ Sodium reacts violently with water. These bubbles are caused by the production of hydrogen gas.

▶ **Calcium** will also react with cold water, but much less violently than the alkali metals. The chemical equation for this reaction is:

Calcium ✚ Water ⟶ Calcium hydroxide ✚ Hydrogen

$$Ca_{(s)} + 2H_2O_{(l)} \longrightarrow Ca(OH)_{2(aq)} + H_{2(g)}$$

Calcium hydroxide is also soluble and turns universal indicator purple.

▶ **Magnesium** reacts very slowly with cold water, but is much more reactive with steam. To make magnesium react with steam, a coil of ribbon is placed into a test tube with some wet mineral wool and the neck of the tube is closed with a bung. As the test tube is heated, the hydrogen gas escapes through a small hole in the bung.

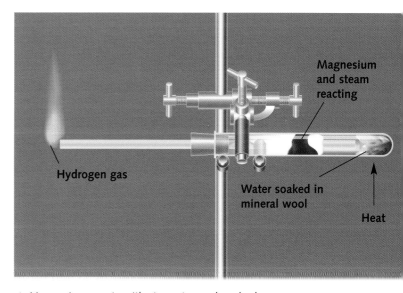

Magnesium and steam reacting

Hydrogen gas

Water soaked in mineral wool

Heat

▲ Magnesium reacts with steam to produce hydrogen.

The equation for this reaction is:

Magnesium ✚ Steam ⟶ Magnesium oxide ✚ Hydrogen

$$Mg_{(s)} + H_2O_{(g)} \longrightarrow MgO_{(s)} + H_{2(g)}$$

Magnesium oxide is a base as well as a metal oxide.

▶ **Zinc** reacts quite slowly with steam. The zinc oxide product is a solid metal oxide (and is a base):

Zinc + Steam ⟶ Zinc oxide + Hydrogen
$$Zn_{(s)} + H_2O_{(g)} \longrightarrow ZnO_{(s)} + H_{2(g)}$$

▶ **Iron** will react very slowly with steam to form solid iron oxide and hydrogen gas. Once more, the iron oxide product is a base:

Iron + Steam ⟶ Iron oxide + Hydrogen
$$2Fe_{(s)} + 3H_2O_{(g)} \longrightarrow Fe_2O_{3(s)} + 3H_{2(g)}$$

Metals that do not react with water include copper and gold. This is why copper is used to make water pipes (see page 10).

REACTIONS OF METALS WITH ACIDS

Water is a weak acid and when metals react with conventional acids, such as hydrochloric acid and sulphuric acid, the reaction is similar but much more vigorous. Magnesium, for example, reacts strongly with hydrochloric acid to produce magnesium chloride and hydrogen gas.

TEST YOURSELF

▶ Predict the name of the following metal and write chemical and word equations to indicate the changes that have occurred:

This metal will only react with water in the presence of steam to form a metal oxide and hydrogen gas. The reaction rate is fast.

IRON AND OXYGEN

When metals such as aluminium and silver are exposed to the air, they lose their shine because a layer of oxide forms on the surface. This layer protects the metal beneath and prevents further reactions. This is called tarnishing or **oxidation**. However, metals such as iron are not so lucky. When iron is left in the presence of oxygen and water, the metal begins to rust. Parts of the metal gradually fall away and the iron beneath becomes weakened. Rust is an example of corrosion that causes metal to wear away. However, the term 'rust' only refers to iron (or alloys, such as steel, that have a high iron content).

▲ The iron components of this van are wearing away because they have become corroded by rust.

HOW DOES RUST FORM?

Rust forms when water from the air **condenses** onto the surface of a piece of iron, allowing dissolved oxygen gas from the air to attack the iron atoms on the surface. The oxygen and iron react together to form iron (III) oxide (one of a number of types of iron oxide). This has a brown flaky appearance and the formula is Fe_2O_3.

During the oxidation of iron, electrons are transferred between the atoms causing an **electrochemical reaction**. This chemical change is capable of releasing an electrical charge. The reaction can also be speeded up if conduction is improved. This is what happens by the sea where the air contains a lot of dissolved salt (sodium chloride) from the seawater. The presence of salt increases the rate at which electrons move around, and rust forms more quickly. People who live near the sea often find that their cars rust more quickly than the cars of friends who live further inland.

HOW CAN WE PROTECT IRON FROM RUSTING?

The formation of rust can cost millions of pounds every year so it is important to stop rust from occurring in the first place. Once rust has formed, it is difficult to treat. Rust is commonly prevented in one of the following ways.

▶ **Plastic** – Garden furniture made from steel is often covered in plastic to prevent oxygen and water from reaching the metal. The plastic coating means that the furniture can be left outside all year round, with a reduced risk of rusting.

▲ Garden furniture is often coated with plastic to prevent it from rusting when it is left outside.

▶ **Galvanising** – The steel tins that store our food do not rust because they have been coated with a less reactive metal, such as zinc. Zinc will not corrode in the presence of oxygen and water, and will therefore protect the steel underneath. Metal dustbins are also treated in this way.

▶ **Painting** – When iron is painted, water and oxygen cannot get to the metal. This method is used to protect our cars. It works very well until the paintwork is damaged (even slightly). If water and oxygen get in, rust forms beneath the paintwork. This kind of rust has a characteristic 'pitted' appearance.

▶ **Oil or grease** – Oil or grease can be used to protect tools and machinery from rusting. This works in the same way as paint, by preventing water and oxygen from reaching the iron.

▶ **Sacrificial protection** – Steel ships are protected by bars of magnesium which are attached to the side of the ship. Because magnesium is more reactive than iron (see page 18) it will corrode instead of the iron. The magnesium bars are replaced when they are nearly corroded for maximum protection.

The reactivity series

3

The reactions of metals with acids, water and oxygen provide us with clues about the reactivity of different metals. Other clues come from where the metals were actually found. Reactive metals are generally found as ores because they chemically combine with other elements. These metals can only be extracted using chemical techniques. Other metals, such as gold and platinum, are found on their own (or in their 'native' form). We know that these metals are un-reactive because they have not become chemically combined.

THE REACTIVITY SERIES

The order of a metal's reactivity can be found by looking at the **reactivity series**. This list was arranged by observing a series of reactions and putting the metals in order of their readiness to react with substances, such as oxygen, water and acids.

The reactivity series helps us to understand more about the properties of different metals and to predict how metals might behave. Thanks to the reactivity series, for example, we now know that the more reactive a metal is, the more stable its compounds are likely to be.

DISPLACEMENT REACTIONS

When two elements react together, the more reactive element will displace the less reactive element from its compound. We call this a **displacement reaction**. Displacement reactions are useful because they provide us with clues about the reactivity of different metals.

When a piece of copper is placed into a solution of silver nitrate, for example, the copper begins to react with the silver compound. A number of visible changes can be observed during this reaction. The colourless silver nitrate solution begins to turn slightly blue and the copper gains

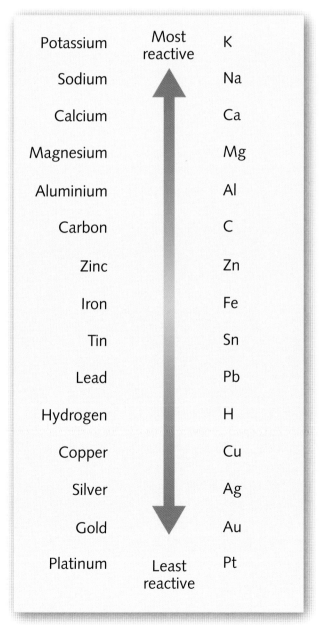

▲ This reactivity series shows the reactivity of common metals in comparison to carbon and hydrogen.

a heavy deposit of a silver-coloured metal. The equation for this reaction is:

$$Copper + Silver\ nitrate \longrightarrow Copper\ nitrate + Silver$$

$$Cu_{(s)} + Ag_2NO_{3(aq)} \longrightarrow CuNO_{3(aq)} + 2Ag_{(s)}$$

The blue solution is copper nitrate and the metal deposit is pure silver that has been displaced from the silver nitrate solution. Because copper is more reactive than silver it has the effect of knocking silver out of its compound.

REACTIVITY WITH WATER, ACID AND OXYGEN

We have seen that group 1 metals react vigorously with water, whilst others, such as copper, are completely un-reactive (see chapter 2). The same trend is observed with metal-acid reactions because water is a very weak acid. We also know that group 1 metals are very reactive with oxygen in the atmosphere – we have to store them under oil. At the same time,

other metals, such as platinum, resist reaction completely. This relative order of reactivity is reflected in the reactivity series.

MAKING PREDICTIONS

We know from experiments (and the reactivity series) that the most reactive metals are more likely to form compounds. They also have the greatest chance of displacing a less reactive metal. When two metals are in competition with each other, we call the reaction that takes place a competition reaction.

For example, imagine we put a sample of zinc into a copper sulphate solution. Zinc is more reactive than copper so when these metals are put into competition with each other, we would expect the zinc to displace the copper from its compound. When this experiment is conducted, the silvery metal is replaced by a dark-coloured solid and the solution loses its blue colour.

◀ Copper sulphate is bright blue (left), but when it reacts with a more reactive metal, such as zinc, the copper is displaced from its salt, and appears as a dark or reddish-brown copper metal (right).

An equation for this reaction is:

Zinc + Copper sulphate $\longrightarrow$ Zinc sulphate + Copper

$$Zn_{(s)} + CuSO_{4(aq)} \longrightarrow ZnSO_{4(aq)} + Cu_{(s)}$$

But this reactivity will not work the other way around. If we try to react copper and zinc sulphate together, there is no reaction. Zinc is already in a chemical compound, and as the more reactive metal, this is unlikely to change.

The reactivity series is a vital tool for chemists. It helps us to understand the properties of metals and the differences between them. It also helps us to make predictions about a metal's behaviour based on knowledge of its position in the table. This is particularly useful when determining the best method for extracting a metal from its ore (see chapter 4). The method of extraction used depends upon the position of the metal in the reactivity series.

▲ No reaction occurs with copper in a zinc sulphate solution.

TEST YOURSELF

▶ Look at the following combinations and predict whether a reaction will occur or not. If you think a reaction will occur, write a chemical equation for the changes that take place.

(1) Tin and magnesium sulphate
(2) Iron and silver sulphate
(3) Lead and copper sulphate

DID YOU KNOW?

▶ When aluminium reacts with iron oxide it produces a lot of heat. The equation for this reaction is:

Aluminium + Iron oxide $\longrightarrow$ Aluminium oxide + Iron

$$2Al_{(s)} + Fe_2O_{3(s)} \longrightarrow Al_2O_{3(s)} + 2Fe_{(l)}$$

The heat is sufficient to melt the iron product and is useful for welding reactions. When the iron forms, it can be poured into gaps in train tracks (right), for example, to weld them together. This is called a thermite reaction.

▶ A displacement reaction is used to extract bromine from seawater. Seawater contains sodium bromide in solution. By treating the seawater with chlorine gas, bromine can be extracted in the following reaction:

Chlorine + Sodium bromide $\longrightarrow$ Sodium chloride + Bromine

$$2NaBr_{(aq)} + Cl_{2(g)} \longrightarrow 2NaCl_{(aq)} + Br_{2(l)}$$

Bromine is one of the few liquid elements. It is used in flame retardants for domestic and industrial purposes. Bromine can also be used in pesticides. Since seawater contains 65 parts per million (ppm) bromine, the sea is a potential source of around 100 trillion tonnes of bromine!

Extraction techniques

4

Study the reactivity series carefully (see page 18) and locate metals that you believe have been around for a long time. Can you see any patterns? The metals that were first discovered tend to be near the bottom of the reactivity series. This is because the less reactive metals, such as iron and copper, are the easiest to extract. More modern metals, such as aluminium and titanium, only began to be extracted from their ores in the late 1800s, thanks to the discovery and development of electricity.

Many of the most precious metals have been known about for thousands of years. Ancient civilisations, such as the Old Kingdom in Egypt (about 3000 BCE) used gold for decoration. Gold is a very un-reactive metal and is found in its native form. Other civilisations made use of different metals – in the 'Iron Age' (approximately 800 BCE) and the 'Bronze Age' (approximately 1800 BCE) for example. Bronze is an alloy composed mainly of copper. Both iron and copper are also relatively un-reactive metals. They have been easily extracted and used for many years.

METALS OF MEDIUM REACTIVITY

Metals that are found in ores (and are below carbon in the reactivity series) rely on roasting techniques for their extraction (see page 25). An example of this is iron ore (or **haematite**). When haematite is reacted with carbon monoxide gas, the following reaction occurs:

Iron oxide (haematite) + Carbon monoxide
⟶ Iron + Carbon dioxide

$$Fe_2O_{3(s)} + 3CO_{(g)} \longrightarrow 2Fe_{(s)} + 3CO_{2(g)}$$

Carbon monoxide is produced when carbon dioxide reacts with carbon. Because carbon monoxide has a greater affinity for oxygen at these temperatures than iron, it displaces the compound in this example to make carbon dioxide.

▶ The Egyptians used gold for many of their decorative items.

All the metal ores found below carbon in the reactivity series can be extracted in a similar way. They were discovered long ago because there was always a plentiful supply of carbon – from wood, coal, dead organisms and from fires used for heating.

▲ In the 1600s, silver was separated from black copper ores using large furnaces.

▲ A worker sifts bauxite dust during the production of aluminium, which costs almost ten times more than iron to produce.

METALS OF HIGH REACTIVITY

Metals above carbon in the reactivity series cannot be extracted from their ores using roasting techniques. If we try to combine compounds of metals of high reactivity with carbon, no reaction takes place. **Bauxite**, for example, is an ore containing mostly aluminium oxide. Carbon cannot react with aluminium oxide because, as the more reactive element, aluminium is already in a compound. Instead, metals of high reactivity are extracted from their ores using a technique called **electrolysis** (see page 29).

DID YOU KNOW?

▶ In 1576, the English explorer Martin Frobisher brought a shiny rock back from Baffin Island, Canada. The rock was confirmed to be gold and many explorers grew excited about the possibilities on Baffin Island. Many dangerous and hard explorations followed, but when almost 2,000 tonnes of the material had been retrieved, it was examined more closely and found to be a mixture of iron ore and sulphur. Today, this substance is called 'fools gold'.

▶ During the 1800s, many people in the USA travelled to the West Coast because they heard there was a lot of gold to be found there. The fact that gold needed no extraction and was worth a lot of money was too good to resist. However, because gold is quite rare, the supply quickly became exhausted leaving many people disappointed. Today, the price of gold still remains high due to its rarity.

▲ An explorer pans for gold in Northern California, USA (tinted photograph, circa 1890).

In the 1700s, scientists began to experiment to create different types of electricity. Today, the extraction of many metals relies upon advanced electrochemical techniques. Here we look at three historical figures who stand out as making important contributions to the discovery and development of electrochemistry.

JOSEPH PRIESTLEY (1733-1804)

Joseph Priestley was a British chemist (and also a philosopher, a clergyman and a teacher). Priestley is perhaps best known for his discovery of oxygen. However, as part of his work, Priestley also spent time studying electricity. He was the first to discover that carbon conducts electricity, for example. Carbon is now commonly used in batteries and for electrolysis (see page 29).

ALESSANDRO VOLTA (1745-1827)

Alessandro Volta was an Italian scientist. He worked as a professor of physics and had a particular interest in electricity.

In 1800, Volta invented the voltaic pile – the first electric battery. At the time, electricity was hardly known about and Volta became very excited by his findings. Volta made a

▲ Alessandro Volta

stack of alternating layers of zinc metal, absorbent paper soaked in salty water, and silver metal. Volta had worked out that zinc and silver were such dissimilar metals that they would react to produce the greatest amount of electricity.

The voltaic pile worked on the principle that if two metals touch in water, one metal dissolves in a chemical reaction that drives electricity around the circuit. When Volta attached a wire to the top and bottom of his voltaic pile, he produced an electrical current. And if the voltaic pile got taller in size, a stronger current was produced.

The Daniell cell soon followed the invention of the voltaic pile. This type of battery was commonly used for doorbells in the 1800s. The cell consists of copper and zinc plates in copper sulphate and zinc sulphate solutions.

The copper is placed at the bottom and copper sulphate is poured into the top, half filling the jar. The zinc plate is then hung half way through the jar and zinc sulphate is poured very carefully over the top. The zinc sulphate floats because it is less dense than copper sulphate. This battery worked well as long as it stayed in one position – if the battery moved, the chemicals became mixed up.

▲ The Daniell cell was invented in 1836.

HUMPHRY DAVY (1778-1829)

Humphry Davy was another British chemist who experimented with electricity. From the work of previous scientists, Davy recognised that some substances could be split into their individual elements using electricity. At the time, substances such as potash (potassium oxide) and lime (calcium oxide) were thought to consist of different elements but no one had successfully split them apart. Davy built a very large battery and then heated both potash and lime until they were molten. When he passed an electrical current through the potash he discovered tiny, shiny pieces of metal that caught on fire when placed in water. This was potassium. Davy had successfully discovered electrolysis and went on to separate elements such as sodium, calcium and magnesium from their compounds.

▶ BUILD YOUR OWN VOLTAIC PILE

(Note: You should ask an adult's permission before conducting this experiment).

(1) Mix a strong solution of salt and water (so the water cannot hold any more salt).

(2) Soak strips of absorbent paper (such as a paper towel) in the saltwater solution.

(3) Create a voltaic pile by stacking the absorbent paper between copper and silver-coloured coins.

(4) You can buy an inexpensive voltmeter from a DIY shop (or use one from your school). Place the wires from the voltmeter at each end of your stack and measure the voltage that is being produced.

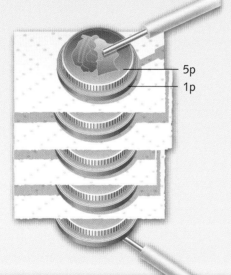

5p
1p

▶ OTHER WAYS TO PRODUCE ELECTRICITY

(1) Make two slits in the skin of a lemon and insert a piece of aluminium foil into one slit and a copper nail into the other. The metals should not touch each other inside the lemon.

(2) Attach the wires from a voltmeter to each metal and measure the voltage that is produced. A current flows because a chemical reaction takes places between the metals and the acid in the lemon juice.

(3) Put the aluminium and copper into a beaker of fresh water and then a beaker of saltwater. Are there any changes to the voltage? You can also experiment using different metal objects, such as coins. Which combination of metal objects and solutions gives the highest voltage?

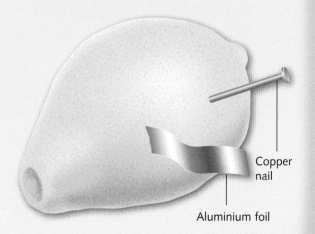

Copper nail

Aluminium foil

DID YOU KNOW?

▶ Experiments using dissected frogs' legs led to the development of the voltaic pile. Alessandro Volta discovered that dissected frogs' legs twitched when two different metals touched them. This was caused by an electric current flowing between the metals.

▶ Thanks to the initial work of scientists in the 1700s and 1800s, the development of electrochemical techniques now have applications in space. Some

satellites and space stations are powered by solar panels that generate electricity when sunlight falls on them. However, for times when there is no direct sunlight, the energy needs to be stored. In space stations, water is split to make hydrogen and oxygen gases that can be stored and later combined in a **fuel cell** to generate electricity. Satellites do not have as much room for storage, so instead use rechargeable batteries.

Extracting iron, aluminium and copper

5

Iron, aluminium and copper are metals that have many everyday uses, but their extraction is not always easy. Today, metal extraction techniques have become big business around the world. Here we take a look at the common extraction processes of these three metals.

GETTING THE IRON OUT

Iron has been extracted from its ore, haematite, for hundreds of years using a simple roasting technique. The same principles apply today, but roasting occurs in a special furnace called a **blast furnace**. Let's take a journey through a blast furnace to find out the important chemical changes that occur.

A BLAST FURNACE

(1) The raw materials

Haematite, coke, limestone and hot air are the raw materials used in a blast furnace in the production of iron. Haematite is an iron ore and is mostly composed of the compound iron (III) oxide (Fe_2O_3). Coke is a form of carbon that is derived from coal. It is much cheaper than using a pure and refined form of carbon.

Limestone is a compound called calcium carbonate ($CaCO_3$). This compound is extracted through limestone mining – the traditional method of using an explosion to create and collect limestone debris. Hot air is injected into the blast furnace at regular intervals. Oxygen forms approximately 20 per cent of air and is necessary for this process.

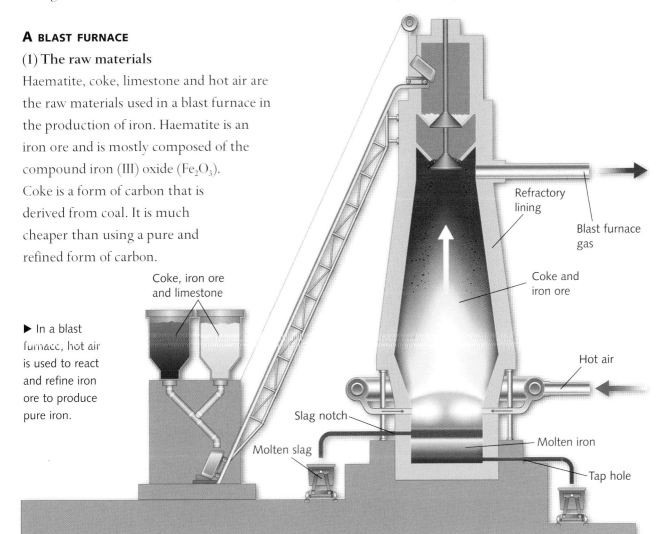

▶ In a blast furnace, hot air is used to react and refine iron ore to produce pure iron.

Coke, iron ore and limestone

Refractory lining

Blast furnace gas

Coke and iron ore

Hot air

Slag notch

Molten slag

Molten iron

Tap hole

▲ This molten iron has been tapped from a blast furnace and will be used to make steel.

(2) The first reactions

Limestone, haematite and coke together are called the **charge**. The charge is lowered into the furnace where the temperature is about 1,000°C. The heat is sufficient to cause the carbon in the coke to react with oxygen in the following way:

Carbon + Oxygen $\longrightarrow$ Carbon dioxide

$$C_{(s)} + O_{2(g)} \longrightarrow CO_{2(g)}$$

This reaction releases lots of heat and helps to keep the furnace at a high temperature. At regular intervals, another blast of air is introduced into the furnace using large bellows.

The carbon dioxide then reacts with further coke from the charge in the following way:

Carbon dioxide + Carbon $\longrightarrow$ Carbon monoxide

$$CO_{2(g)} + C_{(s)} \longrightarrow 2CO_{(g)}$$

The carbon monoxide then reacts with haematite in a displacement reaction to give pure iron:

Carbon monoxide + Iron oxide $\longrightarrow$ Carbon dioxide + Iron

$$3CO_{(g)} + Fe_2O_{3(s)} \longrightarrow 3CO_{2(g)} + 2Fe_{(s)}$$

Carbon monoxide is described as a **reducing agent** because it reduces the iron oxide to pure iron. It does this by removing oxygen from the iron oxide in a competition reaction (see page 19).

(3) Extracting the iron

The pure iron forms near the bottom of the furnace because the original haematite is quite heavy and sinks into the furnace. At this level, the temperature is approximately 2,000°C – sufficient to melt the iron. Molten iron falls to the bottom of the furnace and is tapped off immediately for steel production.

The molten iron is treated straight away to save the energy needed to re-melt it. The carbon dioxide produced during this process remains in the furnace and is used again in step (2).

Notice how more gas is produced than is used up in these three steps. It would be dangerous for the furnace to be completely enclosed because the gas pressure would build up and cause an explosion. To prevent this from happening, waste gas escapes through vents at the top of the furnace. The waste gases are sometimes released into the atmosphere.

WHAT IS THE LIMESTONE USED FOR?

Haematite is mostly iron (III) oxide but it also contains some impurities (such as silicon dioxide). If these impurities remained in the iron product, it would cause brittleness. Limestone (calcium carbonate) is used to remove the silicon impurities. The first of these reactions is called a thermal decomposition of limestone. Limestone forms two products in the heat of the furnace:

Calcium carbonate (limestone) $\longrightarrow$
Calcium oxide + Carbon dioxide
$$CaCO_{3(s)} \longrightarrow CaO_{(s)} + CO_{2(g)}$$

The calcium oxide then reacts with the silicon impurities to form a waste product called slag.

The molten slag falls to the bottom of the furnace where it can be tapped off. Molten iron and molten slag are kept separate from each other because they have different densities and therefore fall to different levels. Although slag is a waste product, it can be sold for other uses (for example, as the foundation material for roads and buildings). This helps to make the industrial process more economical.

MAKING CAST IRON

The iron produced in a blast furnace contains about four per cent carbon and is quite brittle. We call it pig iron. Melting the iron at a particular temperature reduces the silicon and carbon content slightly to produce cast iron. Cast iron still contains about two per cent carbon. However, it is more resistant to corrosion than pig iron.

▲ These gears are used in farming machinery. They are made from cast iron which is strong and resists corrosion.

MAKING WROUGHT IRON

Wrought iron is even stronger, but takes a long time to make. Ingots of pig iron are stacked and heated. The iron is then beaten with a hammer, rolled, cut into lengths and stacked again. The quality of the iron improves each time the process is repeated as more carbon is removed. Wrought iron can be shaped without breaking and is often used to make decorative gates, chains and railings. However, many of these products are now made from steel which is easier to manufacture.

DID YOU KNOW?

▶ Blast furnaces do not cool down for almost a year. Charge is constantly fed into the top, and molten slag and molten iron are tapped off at the bottom. The furnace will be 'shut down' for only a couple of weeks each year for maintenance and repair. It is important for manufacturers of iron to operate their blast furnaces at safe temperatures and pressures to avoid dangerous fires.

▲ The Verrazano-Narrows Bridge connects Brooklyn to Staten Island. It is currently the longest suspension bridge in the USA. In summer, the roadway is 30 cm lower than in winter because the steel cables expand and contract in hot and cold weather.

MAKING STEEL

Steel is produced through the BOS making process (Basic Oxygen Steel-making process). Most of the molten pig iron from a blast furnace is pumped into another furnace for steel-making. In the BOS process, a large ladle stirs the molten iron and at the same time delivers a supply of fresh oxygen gas. The carbon impurity reacts with the oxygen to produce carbon dioxide, which escapes from the top of the furnace. Other impurities form a layer of waste on top of the molten iron that can be scraped off.

WHAT ARE THE DIFFERENT TYPES OF STEEL?

There are two main types of steel. Carbon steels are based on the metal iron, with varying amounts of carbon removed by the BOS process. Alloy steels have particular metals added to them to give the steel distinctive properties.

CARBON STEELS

Carbon steels are graded as low, medium or high, depending on their carbon content. Low-grade carbon steels are used for car bodies, medium-grade carbon steels make good railway lines and high-grade carbon steels are used for razor blades and sharp knives.

ALLOY STEELS

Many transition metals (see page 10) are used to make alloys because their properties contribute to the final product. Stainless steel, for example, contains chromium, nickel and iron. It is used for cutlery because it is light and strong and does not tarnish easily. Vanadium steel only contains about two per cent vanadium but it is strong and hard and used to make tools. Molybdenum steel contains about four per cent molybdenum. It is hard-wearing and used to make gun barrels.

EXTRACTION OF ALUMINIUM

Aluminium is the most plentiful metal in the Earth's crust, but it costs approximately ten times more than iron because it is difficult to extract. **Recycling** aluminium saves about 95 per cent of the energy needed to produce the metal from its ores. Most aluminium reserves are found in rocks that are inaccessible or in clays that are difficult to process. The most common aluminium ore that can be processed is bauxite.

HOW IS ALUMINIUM EXTRACTED?

Aluminium is above carbon in the reactivity series (see page 18) so simple roasting techniques are not sufficient to remove aluminium from its ore. An expensive process called electrolysis is used instead.

(1) The bauxite is treated chemically to remove impurities and to leave pure aluminium oxide.
(2) Molten aluminium oxide is then placed into an electrolysis cell – a large structure with a heat-resistant lining to withstand high temperatures.
(3) The electrolysis cell contains two electrodes.

These are attached to an electrical supply, causing one to become positively charged and the other to become negatively charged. The positive electrode sits in the cell and the negative electrode is contained in the lining of the cell.
(4) Aluminium oxide is an ionic compound. In the cell, positively-charged aluminium atoms (Al^{3+}) are attracted to the negative electrode and negatively-charged oxygen atoms (O^{2-}) are attracted to the positive electrode.
(5) At the negative electrode, the aluminium ions pick up some electrons from the electrical supply and aluminium is formed. At the positive electrode, the oxygen ions give up some electrons and become oxygen gas.
(6) The high temperature (almost 1,000°C) causes the aluminium to melt and fall to the bottom of the cell where it is tapped off for later use.
(7) The oxygen gas reacts with the positively-charged carbon electrode at a high temperature, forming carbon dioxide. Unfortunately, this means that the positive electrode slowly wears away and must be replaced every few months.

▼ Aluminium is produced from bauxite using the Bayer process (left) and the Hall-Heroult process (right).

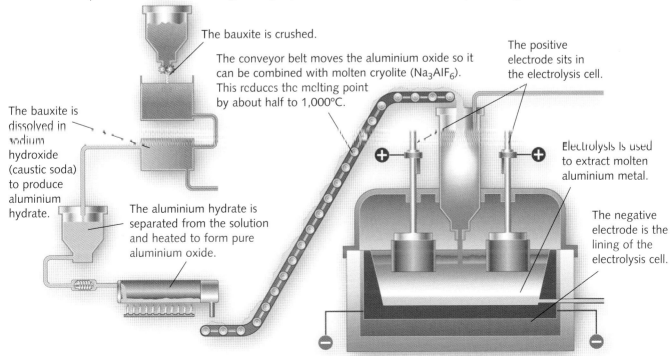

The bauxite is crushed.

The conveyor belt moves the aluminium oxide so it can be combined with molten cryolite (Na_3AlF_6). This reduces the melting point by about half to 1,000°C.

The positive electrode sits in the electrolysis cell.

The bauxite is dissolved in sodium hydroxide (caustic soda) to produce aluminium hydrate.

Electrolysis is used to extract molten aluminium metal.

The aluminium hydrate is separated from the solution and heated to form pure aluminium oxide.

The negative electrode is the lining of the electrolysis cell.

THE EXTRACTION OF COPPER

After iron, copper is the second most commonly used metal in the world. Approximately seven million tonnes of copper are produced each year. Most of this comes from the ores malachite or chalcopyrite, but a small proportion is made from recycled scrap metal. Malachite is mined in the USA, Peru, Zambia and Chile (amongst other countries) from surface mines. Copper's position in the reactivity series means that it can be extracted from its ore using a roasting technique. The extracted copper is then processed using electrolysis to make it as pure as possible.

▲ Malachite's distinctive bright green colour (left) is useful in locating copper deposits. Chalcopyrite (right) is less distinctive but is the most common of the copper ores.

HOW IS COPPER PRODUCED?

The copper ore is extracted from the ground and fed into a large machine for crushing. This machine is a large rotating drum made from steel that crushes the ore into a fine powder. Crushing is necessary because copper ore may contain as little as 0.5 per cent copper, which can only be extracted if a fine powder is produced. The fine powder is then added to water, detergent and a special chemical that causes the copper ore to float to the surface – this is called **froth flotation**. The powder at the top is skimmed off and dried and the copper ore is roasted at a high temperature to produce molten copper.

HOW IS COPPER PURIFIED?

When copper is extracted it can be made into alloys (for use in coins, for example), but it needs to be purified before it can be used for electrical wiring. This is achieved through electrolysis.

Two copper electrodes are used in the electrolysis. The positively-charged electrode (the anode) is a relatively pure copper produced from roasting. The negatively-charged electrode (the cathode) is a much purer copper that has already gone through the electrolysis process. The electrolyte is a copper sulphate solution that is rich in copper ions (Cu^{2+}).

When the electricity is switched on, the copper ions from the electrolyte are attracted to the negatively-charged electrode (because opposite charges attract).

▲ The Chuquicamata copper mine in Chile, South America, is the largest in the world in terms of both size and production. This molten copper will be processed to produce 99.9 per cent pure copper 'cathodes'.

The copper ions pick up two electrons and form copper atoms on the surface of the negative electrode. Meanwhile, the copper atoms from the positively-charged electrode lose two electrons to form copper ions (which replace those lost from the solution). The overall effect of the electrolysis is that the negatively-charged electrode gets larger as fresh copper is deposited onto it, whilst the positively-charged electrode gets smaller.

WHAT HAPPENS TO THE IMPURITIES?

The copper that undergoes this purification also contains other metals. As the electrolysis proceeds, these metals fall to the bottom of the electrolysis cell where they form sludge. Sludge contains many precious metals, such as silver and gold, and can therefore be sold to jewellers and other producers. This makes the purification of copper more cost effective.

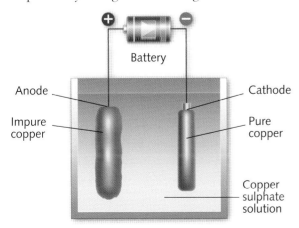

Battery

Anode

Impure copper

Cathode

Pure copper

Copper sulphate solution

▲ Pure copper can be produced using electrolysis.

DID YOU KNOW?

▶ In 2006, copper was priced at an all time high of approximately US$7,000 a tonne. The rise was thought to be a result of the growing demand for copper in developing nations. A rise in copper prices can mean that coins (such as the one cent coin in the USA) are worth less than the metal that they are made from. This is less of a problem in the UK because 'copper' coins are actually steel metal with a copper covering.

TIME TRAVEL: RELEASING METALS USING BIOLOGY

There is a mine in southwest Spain that has been the source of copper ore for almost 2,000 years. For most of this time, the ore was extracted using traditional mining methods, but in the 1700s, engineers noticed a stream of blue-green liquid oozing from the mountains surrounding the site. This liquid ran over old iron tools, leaving a brown film behind. The engineers quickly realised that what they were looking at was actually copper. Copper compounds often have a blue-green colour and the metal itself is pinkish-red.

◄ These copper bars (left) are being stored for further industrial processing. Copper is pinkish-red in colour, but many of its compounds (such as copper carbonate, above) are blue-green.

The engineers were unable to explain the presence of the copper liquid coming from the mountainside and they had little knowledge of micro-organisms. In fact, they believed the copper was produced from the remains of unknown chemical reactions during the mining process. It was not until the 1900s that scientists from the USA discovered that bacteria were actually carrying out this chemical reaction.

WHICH MICRO-ORGANISMS WERE INVOLVED?

The scientists identified the bacteria as *Thiobacillus ferro-oxidans* and *Thiobacillus thio-oxidans*. These bacteria are special because they obtain the energy they need for survival by converting sulphide ions into sulphur atoms.

Sulphide ions are present in copper mines as well as in the **tailing** ponds located near to the mines. When the bacteria convert the sulphide ions to sulphur atoms, the copper atoms to which they were originally attached are released and can be collected. We call this type of biological extraction **biohydrometallurgy**. It is kinder to the environment than traditional copper processing methods. Copper processing plants need to operate at high temperatures, are very polluting and require a great deal of energy. Sulphur dioxide gas is also released during this artificial process. This can dissolve in rain clouds and contribute to **acid rain** – a serious environmental problem.

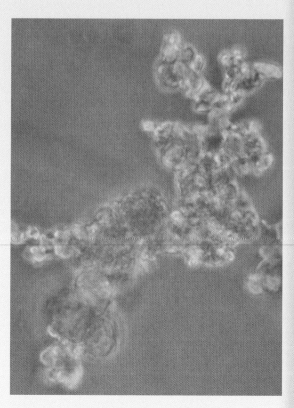

▲ *Thiobacillus ferro-oxidans* bacteria convert sulphide ions into sulphur atoms (magnification x 500).

▲ The coloured pools of water in these ponds contain copper tailings – the waste rock from which copper ore has been removed after mining.

THE ADVANTAGES OF BIOHYDROMETALLURGY

In the mid-1980s, the copper industry in the USA was suffering from a lack of good quality ore because supplies had been exhausted. To meet demands, producers began mining in more obscure locations, and extracting more rock before a suitable ore was found. This caused the cost of production to rise to between US$130 and US$200 per kilo of copper. With the introduction of biohydrometallurgy, however, the price fell to US$70 per kilo and sulphur dioxide emissions were also largely reduced.

HOW IS BIOHYDROMETALLURGY USED?

To extract copper using biohydrometallurgy the low-grade ore and tailings left from traditional mining techniques are piled together into a heap on an area of **impermeable** ground. Bacteria are then sprayed onto the heap in an acidic solution. The bacteria work well in acidic conditions and begin to convert the sulphide ions to sulphur atoms. Because the copper does not sink into the impermeable ground, it can be drained off from the bottom of the pile.

WHAT ARE THE DISADVANTAGES?

Mining companies have not always been keen to use micro-organisms to extract their products because the process is slow and it takes a while to become commercially successful. The method has been applied in areas where high-grade ore has been exhausted, but the slow rate of this process is a serious disadvantage. Traditional mining methods can recover the metal in a matter of months to years – but bacteria can take decades.

DID YOU KNOW?

► Gold extraction is not as straightforward as first believed. Although gold is un-reactive and occurs in its native form, it is often surrounded by a tough compound which needs to be peeled away to release the metal. Bacteria called *Sulpholobus acidocalderius* can help with this process. These bacteria speed up the breakdown of the surrounding material in aqueous conditions at just 70°C. Using this method has increased gold recovery from tricky compounds from 10 per cent to 100 per cent!

6

Alloys

Very few of the metals that we use in our everyday lives are composed of just one type of metal. Manufacturers are far more likely to mix metals together so that they can combine the best properties of particular metals. A mixture of metals is called an alloy. Large bridges are made from steel, an alloy composed mainly of iron. Pure iron rusts easily and because it is brittle, it would not be able to withstand the amount of traffic that passes over a bridge. For this reason, we often mix iron with other metals to produce a stronger material that will not rust.

ALLOYING THROUGH HISTORY

Alloying is an important process that has been used for thousands of years. During the 'Bronze Age' for example (see page 21), copper was mixed with tin to make bronze – a hard material that would not corrode. Bronze was used for making weapons as well as ornaments and statues.

▼ Bronze statues become tarnished on their surfaces but are very resistant to additional corrosion.

HOW DOES ALLOYING WORK?

To make an alloy, metals are mixed together when they are molten. These metals do not react together, but form a new extended structure – this is stronger than the original metal.

In a pure metal, all of the metal atoms are the same size. When pressure is applied during stretching, the layers can slide over each other. Eventually, the layers break apart and the metal is broken.

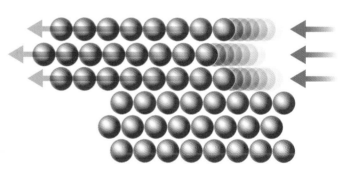

▲ The atoms in this pure metal are arranged in layers that easily slide past each other if a force is applied.

In alloys, this regular, extended arrangement is disrupted by the second metal because it has different-sized atoms. When the metal is now stretched, the larger atoms prevent the layers from slipping past one another and the overall effect is that the material is much stronger.

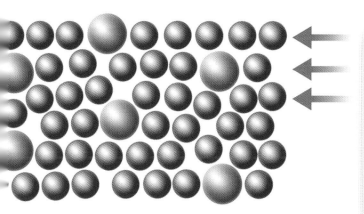

▲ In an alloyed metal, the larger atoms prevent the structure from breaking apart easily.

ALLOYS IN ACTION

There are thousands of different alloys and many more are being invented and produced every day. Some of the more common alloys have the following uses:

▶ **Jewellery** – Precious metals, such as gold, silver and platinum, have become very expensive due to their rarity. However, some of these precious metals can corrode and become worn over time. Gold is alloyed with copper to enhance its strength. Gold alloys have a carat reading to

INVESTIGATE

▶ You will need a shallow dish, a small amount of washing-up detergent and a syringe.
(1) Put some water and detergent into the dish.
(2) Using the syringe, 'inject' a number of similar-sized air bubbles into the dish and observe how they line up.
(3) Now, inject a larger bubble and observe what happens to the pattern. In what ways is this similar to the behaviour of atoms in an alloy?

show how much copper has been added. The higher the carat, the more gold the alloy contains.

▶ **Cutlery** – Traditionally, dining cutlery was made from silver. This is a heavy and expensive metal that is difficult to keep clean. Butlers would polish the cutlery, making it shiny and presentable. Silver has gradually been replaced by stainless steel (an alloy made of iron, chromium and nickel). This alloy is shiny and easy to clean. It is also lighter than silver and does not rust.

▶ The gold in this wedding band has slightly worn away. Gold alloys can be used to make longer-lasting jewellery.

▶ Surgical instruments are made from stainless steel which is strong and easy to keep sterile.

TEST YOURSELF

▶ Find out which metals are used to make the following alloys and explain what properties the final alloys have. What might they be used for?

(1) Duralium
(2) Brass
(3) Solder

▲ Alloys are used to make coins that are hard-wearing, but malleable enough to be stamped with the currency's details.

▶ **Coins** – Alloys are used to make coins so that the value of the coin is greater than the value of the scrap metal. Some coins that look like copper and silver are not pure metals at all. In the UK, for example, copper-coloured coins are a mixture of copper, nickel, zinc and tin. Some silver-coloured coins are a mixture of copper and nickel (and do not contain any silver at all!). A mixture of metals is chosen to ensure that the coins are not easily worn down.

▶ **Medicines** – As we get older, some of the joints in our body suffer from 'wear and tear' and become damaged. When this occurs it may be necessary to replace joints. Artificial joints are traditionally made from metal alloys and plastic. Titanium is the main metal used in these new body parts because it is both light and strong.

7

Carbon & aluminium

Some metals and non-metals have unique properties that make them especially useful for particular purposes. Carbon and aluminium are two examples. Carbon is a non-metal, but has many of the properties sometimes found in metals. One form of carbon (graphite) can conduct electricity. Another form (diamond) is an incredibly hard substance used to make cutting tools or long-lasting jewellery. Aluminium is a metal, but it is extremely light. The fact that aluminium also conducts heat and electricity effectively makes it a very versatile material. Let's look at these two elements in more detail.

CARBON

Carbon's unique strength comes from the way in which the carbon atoms bond together. Some non-metals form many bonds during a chemical reaction. They lose energy during this process but the result is a very stable molecule. When carbon atoms bond, they share electrons to form four bonds between atoms. This type of extended structure can produce three different types of carbon – graphite, diamond and buckminsterfullerene. Elements that can have a different arrangement of atoms like this are called **allotropes**.

(1) GRAPHITE

Graphite is the material found in pencil lead. Although carbon atoms like to form four bonds with each other, in graphite, the carbon atoms form three strong bonds in a hexagonal arrangement. The fourth bonding electron then forms a weak force of attraction between one hexagonal layer and another.

The weaker bond in the extended graphite structure explains some of the unique properties of graphite. Graphite feels smooth and slippery to touch, making it a suitable lubricant for machinery. If the graphite is drawn across a page (such as in a pencil lead), a layer of graphite is left behind. Both of these properties result from pressure being applied to the extended structure. The weak bond between the layers breaks under a firm touch – a pencil line is actually made up of hexagonal layers of carbon atoms.

▲ The hexagonal arrangement of carbon atoms in graphite.

Graphite can conduct electricity because the fourth bonding electron is free to move between the layers of carbon atoms. As it moves, it can carry an electrical charge with it. Graphite is a solid structure because it is composed of thousands of carbon atoms. It also has a high **sublimation** point (3,000°C) at which the graphite turns from a solid straight into a gas.

(2) DIAMOND

In diamond, the carbon atoms are arranged differently to graphite. Each carbon atom is bonded to four other carbon atoms giving a very hard structure. The atoms are also distanced from each other at wide angles (this is called a tetrahedral arrangement).

The bonds between each of the carbon atoms are very strong and the diamond therefore has a high melting point. The bonds between carbon atoms in a diamond are close together, so the resulting

▲ The tetrahedral structure of a diamond molecule.

material is a solid. Diamond is also not soluble in water because the atoms are bonded so tightly together. All of the electrons in the carbon atoms are involved in bonding and are therefore not free to travel around the structure. This means that diamond does not conduct electricity.

(3) BUCKMINSTERFULLERENE

In 1985, scientists working in the UK and the USA discovered the C60 molecule – a molecule containing 60 carbon atoms, arranged as 12 pentagons and 20 hexagons – rather like the pieces of a football. The molecule is miniscule (one nanometre in diameter) and was named Buckminsterfullerene after a famous architect who designed buildings shaped as hemisphere-like domes with this pentagon/hexagon arrangement.

Soon, other members of the fullerene family – such as C70 and C76 – were discovered. Fullerenes are composed entirely of carbon and they are either shaped as a hollow sphere, an oval or a tubular shape. Carbon **nanotubes** belong to the fullerene family, too. These minute tubes are very strong, conduct electricity and are chemically un-reactive. They are now used in some electrical circuit boards. The relatively recent discovery of fullerenes means that new uses are being sought all the time. Some researchers believe they may be a good source of rocket fuel. Others think that their round shape can be useful for delivering medicines to specific parts of the body – the middle of the fullerene could be packed with medicine for delivery.

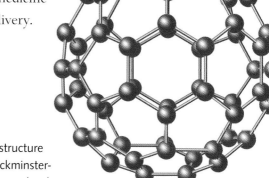

▶ The structure of a buckminster-fullerene molecule.

ALUMINIUM

Metals such as aluminium are considered to be non-renewable resources. Once these metals have been dug up and used, the Earth's natural processes do not replace the mined ores and they will eventually run out. Twelve million tonnes of aluminium are currently used each year. Luckily, aluminium is such a plentiful metal that there is still an estimated 350 years before natural supplies will run out. However, it is important that we recycle metals such as aluminium – to conserve them, but also to save the energy and expense that their extraction demands (see page 29).

Aluminium is a very versatile metal with many uses:

▲ Aircraft manufacturers make use of aluminium's light weight in the alloys that they use.

(1) Aluminium is an un-reactive metal.

Despite its position in the reactivity series (see page 18), aluminium is a relatively un-reactive metal. As soon as aluminium is produced and exposed to the atmosphere, the following chemical reaction occurs:

$$\text{Aluminium} + \text{Oxygen} \longrightarrow \text{Aluminium oxide}$$
$$2Al_{(s)} + 3O_{2(g)} \longrightarrow Al_2O_{3(s)}$$

This reaction forms a 'protective' layer on the surface of the metal. Once formed, no further reaction can occur and the metal beneath is protected. This means that aluminium appears to have little reactivity (although a reaction has actually occurred). Aluminium's apparent lack of reactivity means that it is ideally suited for use outdoors. Garden furniture, and window and door frames, are often made from aluminium.

(2) Aluminium is light.

Aluminium has a low density (2.70 g cm^{-3}). This is unusual for a metal. Although aluminium is not the best metal conductor, its lightness makes it more suitable than other metals for overhead electrical wires. Aluminium will not droop and can be installed relatively easily. Aluminium can be alloyed to combine its light weight with stronger metals, such as copper or titanium. Aircraft made from these alloys need less energy to fly. Other vehicles, such as 'tube trains' are also made from alloys of aluminium. High performance cars are often made from aluminium because its lightness enables them to travel faster. However, aluminium is too expensive to make cars for everyday use and does not have the strength of cars made from steel (which are safer in the event of an impact).

▲ Traditionally, power lines are made from aluminium.

(3) Aluminium is a good conductor of heat and electricity.

Many metals are good conductors of electricity but few are good conductors of heat. Among those metals that can perform both tasks, aluminium is a clear winner. Because aluminium does not break down at high temperatures it is often used in cooking pots and saucepans.

DID YOU KNOW?

▶ Bauxite (an aluminium ore) contains approximately 28 per cent aluminium metal. This high percentage helps to explain why aluminium is the most plentiful metal in the Earth's crust.
▶ When the Wright brothers flew the first aeroplane at Kitty Hawk in 1903, the cylinder block of the engine that powered the craft was made of an aluminium alloy containing eight per cent copper. Today, aluminium alloys are used to make most parts of an aircraft.

(4) Aluminium is malleable and ductile.

Aluminium can be drawn into thin wires and beaten into sheets without breaking. Aluminium foil takes advantage of this property and is useful for cooking purposes.

(5) Aluminium is reflective.

Aluminium is a very shiny metal and is used for the back of headlights in cars. The metal helps the headlights to shine directly in front of the car – the light that naturally travels from the lamp in a sideways direction is reflected off the aluminium surface and travels back towards the road.

▼ This photograph shows the reflective aluminium surfaces on the inside of a car headlamp.

TEST YOURSELF

▶ For each of the following uses of aluminium, what particular properties of the metal are being utilised?

(1) Drinks cans.
(2) Foil blankets for marathon runners.
(3) Racing bicycles.

Metals today

Metal producers go to great lengths to make their products available to consumers. Unfortunately, the mining process can be destructive to the surrounding countryside and atmosphere. Landscapes are scarred, natural habitats are lost and when metals are crushed, large amounts of waste material and dust are created. By recycling metals we can prevent the need for extensive mining. Recycling also reduces our demands on the energy sources needed for metal extraction (such as coal and oil) and prevents the build-up of polluting gases produced during metal processing.

WHAT HAPPENS TO SCRAP METAL?

Metals can be recycled in most areas. Some towns and districts have an organised collection from local homes, while in other areas waste metals can be deposited in a recycling facility. The different types of metals have to be separated before they are treated. Metals such as aluminium may contain impurities, like silicon, which are melted down in the furnace and tapped off separately. Waste gases from this process are cooled and then released into the environment. Scrap steel is processed in a similar way in a separate furnace. The molten metals are reshaped and moulded into desirable products.

▼ Many different types of metals can be recycled.

DID YOU KNOW?

▶ Every day, enough steel and tin cans are used in the USA to make a steel pipe running from Los Angeles to New York and back again.
▶ Steel cans are recycled into a variety of products, including new cans, bicycle frames and even cars.
▶ Recycling just one car saves around 1,100 kilogrammes of iron ore, 635 kilogrammes of coal and 54 kilogrammes of limestone.

THE PROBLEM OF NUCLEAR WASTE

Some metals are more difficult to recycle than others. For example, scrap metals from an old nuclear power station – such as machinery and tools – are contaminated and likely to remain radioactive for thousands of years.

As a short-term solution to the problem of radioactive waste, contaminated materials are stored in strong metal containers or buried underground. Sometimes however, metals with low levels of radiation are introduced to recycling centres – bringing a risk of contamination to recycled products. In the USA, for example, some buildings have had to be destroyed because the steel from which they were constructed was found to have unacceptably high levels of radioactive material in them. Although nuclear power stations are becoming popular again in some countries, many old power stations are also being closed down. In the coming years we need to find better solutions to the problems of storing or recycling radioactive waste materials.

▲ The metals from nuclear power stations have to be treated with care.

Thankfully, however, the majority of the metals that we recycle on a daily basis are unlikely to come into contact with radioactive sources.

THE GOIANA ACCIDENT

If some scrap metal is not carefully handled, it can result in disastrous consequences. This is what happened in Brazil in 1987, for example, when scavengers took part of a radiation therapy machine from an abandoned hospital in Central Brazil. The machine was probably taken for the value of its steel and lead casing and was later sold to a junkyard owner who wanted to make it into jewellery. Unfortunately, the source was highly radioactive and many workers at the junkyard and people living nearby soon became exposed to the radiation.

When it became clear that so many people were getting seriously ill, a sample of dust from the source was taken to a local hospital where it was tested with a radioactive counter. As soon as the danger was realised, an emergency clean-up operation was put into place. During this incident, approximately 100,000 people were examined for radioactive contamination (right) – and over 120 people died.

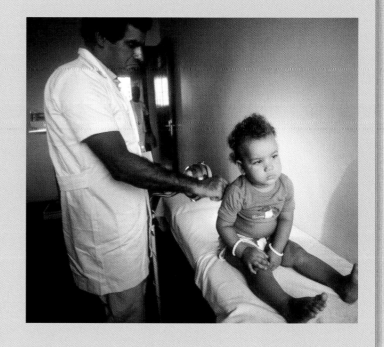

A CLOSER LOOK AT MODERN METALS

Titanium is a transition metal (see page 10). It is a typical metal in its appearance because it looks silvery and metallic and has a relatively low density (4.5 g cm^{-3}). Titanium is as strong as steel but is only about 60 per cent of its density. It is chemically resistant to attack from oxygen and water and is often found in alloys. Its most popular compound is titanium dioxide. Titanium dioxide is found in toothpaste and many other everyday products.

Titanium is a very versatile metal, but its discovery and use is relatively recent. Although the metal was discovered in England in 1791, it was not until 1946 that a commercial process for its extraction was established. Titanium is difficult to extract from its ore and requires a procedure that we call the Kroll Process. During this process, titanium tetrachloride is reacted with magnesium (or sodium) in the following way:

Titanium tetrachloride + Magnesium
$\longrightarrow$ Titanium + Magnesium chloride
$$TiCl_{4(s)} + 2Mg_{(s)} \longrightarrow Ti_{(s)} + 2MgCl_{2(s)}$$

The largest amount of titanium is produced in Australia – approximately 31 per cent of the world total. This is followed by South Africa, Canada, Norway and Ukraine. Titanium is the ninth most plentiful metal in the Earth's crust where it makes up about 0.63 per cent of the Earth's mass.

PROPERTIES AND USES OF TITANIUM

▶ Titanium resists chemical attack by acids, chlorine gas and common solutions. It is excellent for wristwatch casings because it will not easily tarnish when exposed to the air.

▶ Titanium is incredibly light and strong and can withstand extreme temperatures. This makes it an excellent material to use in aircraft and spacecraft. Titanium is often alloyed with aluminium to fulfill this purpose (see page 39). Titanium pipes are also used in offshore oil rigs because of these properties.

▶ Titanium can be alloyed with vanadium. This material is used to make fire-proof walls and hydraulic tubing.

▶ Titanium's lightness is useful for some sports equipment (see page 10). Tennis racquets, and golf clubs are often made from titanium.

▶ Approximately 95 per cent of titanium is used as titanium dioxide, which is a brilliant white colour. Titanium dioxide is used in pigments and paints. Titanium dioxide is also used in sunscreens due to its ability to protect skin by reflecting harmful ultraviolet rays.

▲ Titanium is a common ingredient in many sunscreens.

▶ Titanium has excellent chemical resistance to seawater and can be used to make propeller shafts and divers' knives.

▶ Titanium is chemically un-reactive so it does not react inside the human body. Titanium is therefore used in joint replacements (such as hip joints, and ball and socket joints) and for body piercing parts. Its lightness is also an advantage.

▶ Titanium alloys are also used in glasses frames. This gives a long-lasting and light frame that does not leave an imprint on the nose bridge.

Thanks to our growing understanding of the properties of metals and non-metals, the materials that we are likely to use in the future are going to be more useful than ever before. One growing area of research is the behaviour of **memory metals**. These metals change shape under particular circumstances and can have some interesting applications.

WHAT ARE MEMORY METALS?

Memory metals were first discovered in 1932 when Swedish researcher Arne Ölander studied the properties of a gold-cadmium alloy. This alloy is very expensive, but over the years other alloys have been found to have similar properties. A memory metal is an alloy that 'remembers' its original shape. If the material has been deformed it will regain its original shape when it is reheated or left alone. Today, most memory metals are alloys of nickel, titanium and aluminium or copper.

Memory metals can also adopt two different shapes depending on their temperature. We call these 'smart memory metals'. A force can also be applied to change the shape from one form to another. Another type of memory metals – called ferromagnetic shape memory alloys (FSMA) – change shape under a magnetic field. These materials change shape very quickly and are raising a lot of interest in the research world.

HOW DO MEMORY METALS WORK?

All metals adopt a lattice structure that is regular and closely packed together (see page 7). Memory metals can adopt one of two different crystal structures due to the proportion of different alloying metals that are added. When a smart memory metal is in its lower temperature form, it can usually be bent into different shapes. As the alloy is heated, it transforms into its other state, but it remembers the original crystal structure that it had. On cooling, this structure (and shape) is reformed. Memory metals are described as having a great deal of superelasticity.

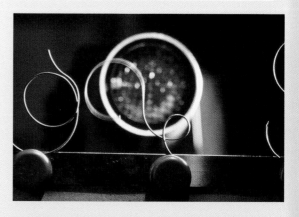

▲ ▼ These photographs show memory metals regaining their original shape when heated. The samples have been manufactured into an 'S' shape. They can be bent with little effort into intricate shapes (above), but will easily regain their shape again after gentle heating (below).

USES OF MEMORY METALS

▶ **Reinforcing arteries and veins.**

Clogged blood vessels can lead to a number of serious health problems. Memory metals with a transition temperature close to body temperature (37°C) can be placed inside locked vessels. The metal will then expand to open up the blockage.

▶ **Fire security.**

Pipes that carry highly flammable and toxic liquids can be programmed with memory metals that shut the system down automatically in the event of a rise in temperature – avoiding potential disaster.

▶ Glasses frames.

Glasses made from memory metals may bend under force, but then retain their original shape (below).

▶ Dental wires.

Braces made from memory metals keep their original shape, despite force and tugging.

▶ Sports equipment.

Sports equipment such as golf clubs can be made partially from memory metals. As the ball comes into contact with the club, the change in shape caused by this force can increase the spin on the ball.

▶ A shape memory metal staple (blue) is mending this ballerina's fractured toe. Here, the staple is trying to return to its original shape (red), holding the two parts of the fractured bone together as they heal.

MEMORY METALS IN THE FUTURE

Shattered bones are usually pinned back together using stainless steel, but scientists say that bones could heal much faster using a different metal alloy. The disadvantage of stainless steel is that it does not hold its shape and bones can move out of place and heal badly. Researchers at Ohio State University in the USA claim that nickel-titanium alloys will help the bones to heal much faster. The alloy is first cooled and then wrapped around the damaged bones. As the alloy heats up to body temperature, it returns to its original shape and exerts a constant pressure on the damaged bones. The researchers used cylinders to represent broken bones and wrapped their alloy around them over a period of six weeks. They found that stainless steel was unable to cope with bone movement but the nickel-titanium alloy performed very well.

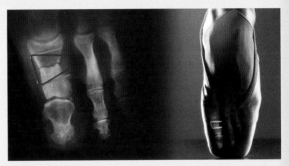

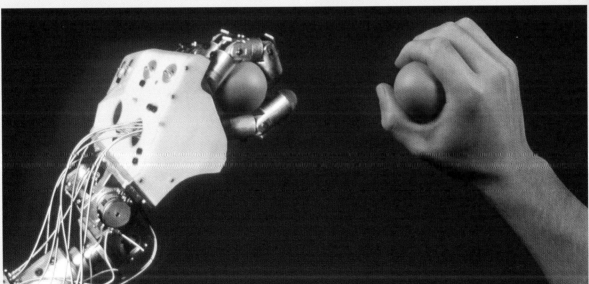

▲ This robot arm (left) has been made with a memory metal. Like the man's hand (right), the robot's fingers are gripping the ball, but when they are released they will smoothly uncurl back to their original position.

Glossary

ACID RAIN – Rain that contains high levels of nitric or sulphuric acid. Acid rain forms when gases from industrial fuels combine with moisture in the atmosphere.

ALLOTROPE – When an element can take more than one form.

ALLOY – A mixture of two or more metals.

AQUEOUS – To contain or be dissolved in water.

BAUXITE – A compound of aluminium and oxygen.

BIOHYDROMETALLURGY – The use of bacteria to perform processes involving metals. For example, the extraction of metals from their ores.

BLAST FURNACE – A large oven used to extract iron from its ore.

BOND – When two or more atoms join together through a chemical reaction.

CATALYST – A substance used to speed up a chemical reaction without itself being used up or changed.

CHARGE – The raw materials fed into a blast furnace.

COMPOUND – A substance consisting of two (or more) elements.

CONDENSE – To change from a gas to a liquid. Condensation occurs when gases are cooled.

CORROSION – The chemical breakdown of a substance.

DENSE – To be very compact. Density is a measure of mass with volume.

DISPLACEMENT REACTION – When a more reactive element replaces a less reactive one from its compound.

DUCTILE – A material that can be drawn into wires.

ANSWERS

p7 Test yourself
(1) Copper is very ductile and a good conductor of electricity.

(2) Steel does not become damaged when hammered.

(3) Aluminium does not react with the drink and can easily be recycled.

p10 Test yourself
(1) Sodium would rapidly react with water in the saucepan and become molten on the stove.

(2) Titanium is very expensive and a lot of metal would be needed.

p12 Test yourself
Astatine molecule – black solid.

p13 Test yourself
Zinc reacts vigorously when burnt in oxygen and zinc oxide quickly forms.

Zinc + Oxygen $\longrightarrow$ Zinc oxide
$2Zn + O_2 \longrightarrow 2ZnO$

p16 Test yourself
Aluminium is the one metal that only reacts with steam.

Aluminium + Steam $\longrightarrow$
Aluminium oxide + Hydrogen
$2Al + 3H_2O \longrightarrow Al_2O_3 + 3H_2$

p17 Investigate
The quickest is air and water, followed by air (because some water from the air will enter); boiled water and cooking oil will not rust

because the former has no oxygen in it and oil prevents the entry of fresh air.

p20 Test yourself
(1) No reaction because magnesium is the more reactive element and will stay in its chemical compound.

(2) A chemical reaction with the formula
$Fe + Ag_2SO_4 \longrightarrow FeSO_4 + 2Ag$

(3) A chemical reaction with the formula
$2Pb + CuSO_4 \longrightarrow Pb_2SO_4 + Cu$

p35 Investigate
The same-sized bubbles will line up in a regular pattern. The larger bubble will disturb the pattern in much the same way as the atoms in an alloy would.

ELECTROCHEMICAL REACTION – A reaction that generates electricity.

ELECTROLYSIS – Using electricity to split up chemical compounds.

ELECTRON – The negative part of an atom.

FROTH FLOTATION – A method of separation.

FUEL CELL – A device, like a battery, that generates electricity via a chemical reaction. Fuel cells use external substances, such as hydrogen and oxygen gas.

HAEMATITE – A compound of iron and oxygen.

IMPERMEABLE – A material that prevents liquids from passing (or diffusing) through it.

INDICATOR – A substance that changes colour in the presence of an acid or an alkali.

MALLEABLE – A material that can be bent into shape.

MEMORY METAL – An alloy that 'remembers' its original shape.

NANOTUBES – Tiny tubes about 10,000 times thinner than a human hair. Nanotubes are made of cylinders of carbon molecules and are the strongest material (for their weight) known to man. Nanotubes are being used in the development of materials.

ORE – A rock containing precious materials or metals.

OXIDATION – A reaction in which oxygen is gained.

PERIODIC TABLE – A table showing all of the chemical elements.

RADIOACTIVE – Matter that gives out radiation.

REACTIVITY SERIES – A series in which metals and other elements are placed in order of their chemical reactivity.

RECYCLING – The process of re-using materials.

REDUCING AGENT – A substance that accepts oxygen in a chemical reaction.

SUBLIMATION – Changing directly from a solid to a gas (or the other way around).

TAILING – The waste remaining after an ore has been processed.

p35 Test yourself
(1) Duralium – 96% aluminium and 4% copper. Light and strong. Example – used for aircraft parts.
(2) Brass – 70% copper and 30% zinc. Hard and does not corrode. Example – used for musical instruments.
(3) Solder – 70% tin and 30% lead. Low melting point. Example – used to join wires and pipes.

p38 Test yourself
Example answers: Solid, hard, high melting point, non-conductor of electricity.

p40 Test yourself
(1) Un-reactive, malleable.
(2) Malleable, conducts heat.
(3) Light in weight.

Useful websites
www.bbc.co.uk/schools
www.chem4kids.com
www.sciencenewsforkids.org
www.newscientist.com
www.howstuffworks.com

Index

Page references in italics represent pictures.

PHOTO CREDITS – *(abbv: r, right, l, left, t, top, m, middle, b, bottom)* **Cover background image** www.istockphoto.com/Robert Kyllo **Front cover images** (tr) www.istockphoto.com /Roman Krochuk (bl) Louie Psihoyos/Corbis **Back cover image** (inset) www.istockphoto.com/Roman Krochuk **p.1** (tr) www.istockphoto.com/Robert Kyllo (bl) Andrew Lambert Photography/Science Photo Library (br) www.istockphoto.com/Marek Slusarczyk **p.2** (b) www.istockphoto.com/Ron Sumners **p.3** (tr) www.istockphoto.com/Jacques Kloppers (b) www.istockphoto.com/Vera Bogaerts **p.4** (tr) www.istockphoto.com/Duncan Walker (tl) www.istockphoto.com/Bradley Mason (br) www.istockphoto.com/Gilles Glod (bl) www.istockphoto.com **p.5** Louie Psihoyos/Corbis **p.6** (tr) www.istockphoto.com/Duncan Tang (bl) www.bigstockphoto.com (br) www.istockphoto.com/Lasure Calgary **p.7** (mr) www.istockphoto.com/ Clay Fowler **p.8** (tr) Ria Novosti/Science Photo Library **p.9** (tl) Andrew Lambert Photography/Science Photo Library (mr) www.istockphoto.com/Roman Krochuk **p.10** (b) www.istockphoto.com **p.11** (mr) www.istockphoto.com/Martina Misar (br) www.istockphoto.com/Eva Serrabassa **p.12** (tl) www.istockphoto.com/Kaycee Craig **p.13** (mr) www.istockphoto.com/Clayton Hansen **p.14** (br) www.istockphoto.com/Joy Fera **p.15** (bl) Andrew Lambert Photography/Science Photo Library **p.16** (br) www.istockphoto. com/Vera Bogaerts **p.17** (tr) www.istockphoto.com/Madeleine Openshaw **p.19** (bl & bm) Andrew Lambert Photography/Science Photo Library **p.20** (tr) Andrew Lambert Photography/ Science Photo Library (bl) www.istockphoto.com/Lise Gagne **p.21** (mr) www.istockphoto.com/Duncan Walker (br) Hulton-Deutsch Collection/Corbis **p.22** (t) Jim Sugar/Corbis (br) Bettmann/Corbis **p.23** (m) Science Photo Library **p.26** (t) Maximilian Stock Ltd/Science Photo Library **p.27** (mr) www.istockphoto.com/Robert Kyllo **p.28** (t) www.istockphoto.com/ Jeremy Edwards **p.30** (bl & br) www.istockphoto.com/Gilles Glod **p.31** (t) Charles O'Rear/Corbis **p.32** (l) Rosenfeld Images Ltd/Science Photo Library (m) Andrew Lambert Photography/Science Photo Library (r) Lester V Bergman/Corbis **p.33** (t) Gerald French/Corbis **p.34** (bl) www.istockphoto.com/Ron Sumners **p.35** (ml) www.istockphoto.com/ Bradley Mason (mr) www.istockphoto.com **p.36** (t) www. istockphoto.com/Marek Slusarczyk **p.37** (bl) www.istockphoto.com **p.39** Louie Psihoyos /Corbis **p.40** (tl) www.istockphoto.com/Jacques Kloppers (mr) Tek Image/Science Photo Library **p.41** (b) www.istockphoto.com/Robert Kyllo **p.42** (tr) www.istockphoto. com/Dale Taylor (br) Karen Kasmauski/Corbis **p.43** (mr) www.istockphoto.com/Jan Tyler **p.44** (tr & mr) Philippe Plailly/Eurelios/Science Photo Library **p.45** (tl, mr & b) Pascal Goetgheluck/Science Photo Library.